SANDWICH GLASS HANDBOOK

BOOKS BY RUTH WEBB LEE

EARLY AMERICAN PRESSED GLASS
Enlarged and Revised

HANDBOOK OF EARLY AMERICAN PRESSED GLASS PATTERNS

SANDWICH GLASS
Enlarged and Revised

SANDWICH GLASS HANDBOOK

VICTORIAN GLASS

VICTORIAN GLASS HANDBOOK

ANTIQUE FAKES AND REPRODUCTIONS
Enlarged and Revised

PRICE GUIDE TO PATTERN GLASS

A HISTORY OF VALENTINES

NINETEENTH-CENTURY ART GLASS

CURRENT VALUES OF ANTIQUE GLASS

LEE AND ROSE

AMERICAN GLASS CUP PLATES

SANDWICH GLASS HANDBOOK

By
RUTH WEBB LEE

LEE PUBLICATIONS

WELLESLEY HILLS ✦ ✦ ✦ MASSACHUSETTS

Ninth Printing

ISBN 0-910872-05-8

IN EXPLANATION

WHOEVER in these United States has felt the inescapable thrill at the sight of a collection of objects that sing in colors, the glittering marvel of the survival, through the years, of such fragile creations, has perforce heard of Sandwich Glass. More human-interest stories have been told—and more misinformation circulated—about the Boston & Sandwich Glass Company than about any other glass factory in America, and perhaps in the world. For years, "Sandwich" applied to glass, has meant much more than the product of the factory that, beginning in 1825, operated at Cape Cod for over threescore years. It is today a generic rather than a specific label.

If the serious student of Sandwich glass in all its phases finds himself confronted with the inadequacy of the available material, it is only fair to remember that the same is true of practically every century-old American industry. Starting as a purely commercial enterprise, with the profit motif uppermost and therefore concerned chiefly with finding or developing a market for an article of everyday use, it cannot be expected that our manufacturing pioneers should have deemed it a sacred duty to write the detailed history of their venture, or to jot down for posterity the full details about what to them, at the time, was merely the everyday routine of their business.

Years of patient research work has revealed the incredible variety and extent of the Boston & Sandwich Glass Company's output during the sixty-three years of operation. Sandwich offers to the antique loving public more desirable collectibles than any other American glass factory—blown, pressed and molded glass in all sorts of forms, colors and designs. You can specialize in one Sandwich line and still be able to spend years in forming your collection.

In Explanation

This Handbook is designed to meet the need of collectors of any or all the fascinating Sandwich patterns. The story of the factory is pictured herein, together with examples of all their types of glass, including known pieces from their royal family—lacy Sandwich. A complete list of pattern tableware, checked against fragment findings taken from the site of the old factory, has been appended, for the benefit of collectors and dealers. An authentic history of the Boston & Sandwich Glass Company may be found in my volume, *Sandwich Glass*.

RUTH WEBB LEE

PATTERNS IDENTIFIED FROM SANDWICH FRAGMENTS

Argus
Arched Grape
Ashburton

Banded Buckle
Barberry
Beaded Acorn
Beaded Circle (Clear and, or, Milk white)
Beaded Grape Medallion (one type)
Beaded Mirror
Bellflower
Bigler
Blackberry (one type, not such fine detail as Wheeling product)
Block with Thumbprint
Bleeding Heart
Bradford Blackberry
Buckle
Bull's Eye and Fleur-de-Lys
Bull's Eye and Bar

Cable
Cable with ring
Colonial
Chrysanthemum Leaf
Comet
Crystal (one type)
Cube

Daisy and Button (very little made at Sandwich)
Diamond Thumbprint

Diamond point
Diamond Quilted with Bull's Eye border
Dickinson
Divided Heart
Drapery

Fine Rib
Flat Diamond and Panel
Flute
Flute with Diamond border
Frosted Leaf
Flowered Oval

Gothic
Grape and Festoon (clear background)
Grape and Festoon (stippled background)
Grape Band Variant
Gooseberry (clear or milk-white)

Hamilton (2 fragments in blue)
Hamilton with leaf
Hobnail (one type)
Horn of Plenty
Huber

Inverted Heart (sauce dishes, honey dishes, bowls, etc.)
Inverted Fern
Inverted Thumbprint (very little made at Sandwich)
Ivy

Patterns Identified From Sandwich Fragments

Leaf and Dart
Lincoln Drape
Loop
Loop and Dart
Loop and Dart, round ornament
Loop and Dart, diamond ornament
Lyre

Magnet and Grape, frosted leaf
Magnet and Grape, stippled leaf

New England Pineapple

Open Rose
Overshot glass

Petal and Loop
Pillar
Powder and Shot
Pressed Block
Prism
Prism and Diamond Point
Pressed Leaf

Rayed, with loop border
Ribbed Acorn
Ribbed Grape
Ripple
Roman Key (clear or frosted)

Sandwich Star
Sawtooth
Scalloped Lines
Smocking
Star and Punty
Stippled Band
Stippled Fuchsia
Stippled Star
Strawberry

Thumbprint (one type, not the earliest)
Tree of Life

Variation of the Pillar

Waffle
Waffle and Thumbprint

SANDWICH GLASS HANDBOOK

PLATE 1
Deming Jarves, founder of the Boston & Sandwich Glass Company.

PLATE 2
Deming Jarves' Model Factory.

PLATE 3

John Jarves (left), for whom the Cape Cod Glass Works was built by his father,
Deming Jarves.

Boston Nov 23. 1825

There is much demand for Lamp
Glasses all kinds. Messrs Summers order—
3 doz 4th size Liverpool L Glass Lips 2 to 2⅛ inch
or nearly to 2¼ inch will answer not too long
a tulip neck
3 doz Mallorys 1¾ inch at lip — 5 holes long small lip
2 doz Globe L Glasses 2 inch at bottom
2 do — do — same shape 1¾ inch a bottom to 1⅝ inch
1 do — do — do inch 1⅞ inch at lip
of any measure over the lips can be weighed
down by wheeler at the lathe—

also recommend your making the following
No — 30 doz No 1 Liverpool L Glasses 2 inch lip ½ Tulip
100 — 30 — " — 2 — 2½ — ½ do
x+ 30 " — 3 — 2¼ — ½
x+ 30 — 4 — 2 — ¾

make them near to this size as possible little
over or under will be of no consequence & do not have
the necks too long they do not appear with proportion
when long — let the bulbs be in proportion to the lip—
50 doz common size bulb 2 inch or any lamp socket
part tulip not too long but a fair proportion
50 doz ½ inch do do 1¾ to 2¼ usual length
size all made light as possible & as many made
each week as convenient — Michael Doyle can make
2 more p week — Snowdon & Haynes for part of the
large size & tell them to have their lips.
Cylinder Rose feet Lamps common & plated cups
are much called for—
at J Hall — Summer & Hay & Atkins have had many of
their rose feet Lamps broke by bad packing Hall

PLATE 4

Specimen of Deming Jarves' handwriting, written with a quill pen, in 1825.

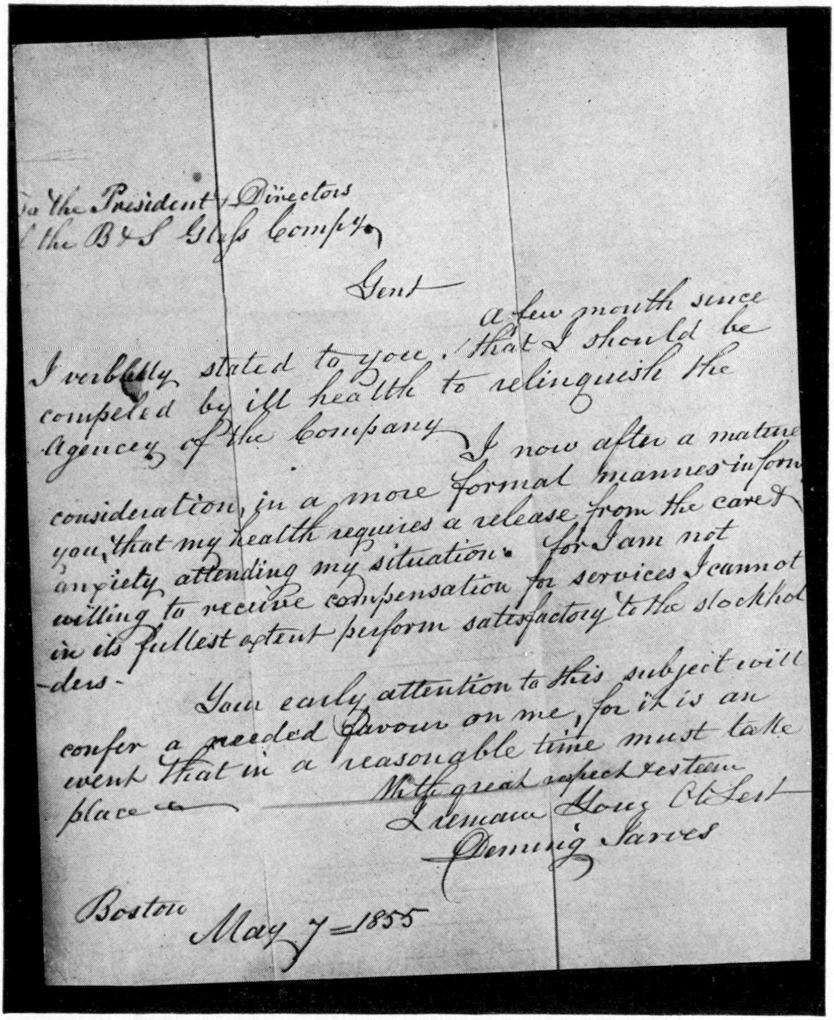

PLATE 5

DEMING JARVES' LETTER OF RESIGNATION

It is dated May 7, 1855, and states that his health requires a release from the cares and anxiety attending his situation. He actually left the company in June, 1858.

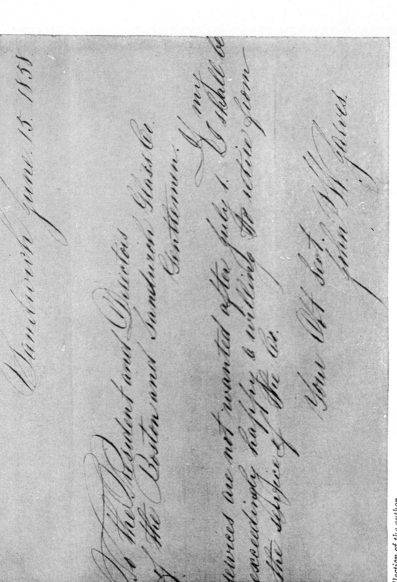

PLATE 6

RESIGNATION OF JOHN W. JARVES

It was for this son that Deming Jarves organized the short-lived Cape Cod Glass Works after both had severed their connection with the Boston & Sandwich Glass Company.

Courtesy of Robert W. Lee

PLATE 7

Deming Jarves' Tombstone. Mt. Auburn Cemetery, Cambridge, Mass.

PLATE 8

THE ORIGINAL RECORD LEDGER

In it, handwritten, are the Act of Incorporation of the Boston & Sandwich Glass Company, its by-laws, and the directors' meetings from the start in 1826 until May 22, 1851. Continuity is preserved in other books until the close of the factory.

PLATE 9

THE STOCK TRANSFER RECORDS

In these two books are written the names and number of shares of the original stockholders, and the transfer of stock to subsequent owners.

PLATE 10

Early view of the Upper House, Sandwich, built in 1849.

PLATE 11

Early view of the Boston & Sandwich Glass Company, creek and dock.

PLATE 12

Upper: "View of Sandwich Glass Works" Wood engraving, drawn from nature, under date of 1836.

Lower: "Boston & Sandwich Glass Company Manufactory. Sandwich, Mass." Dated August 26, 1857.

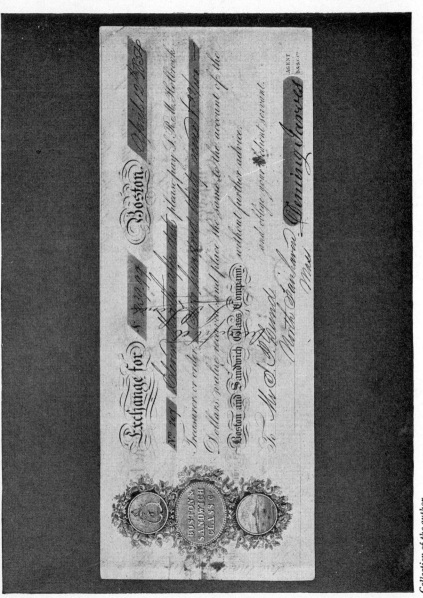

PLATE 13

Bank draft of the Boston & Sandwich Glass Company, signed by Deming Jarves, April 12, 1854.

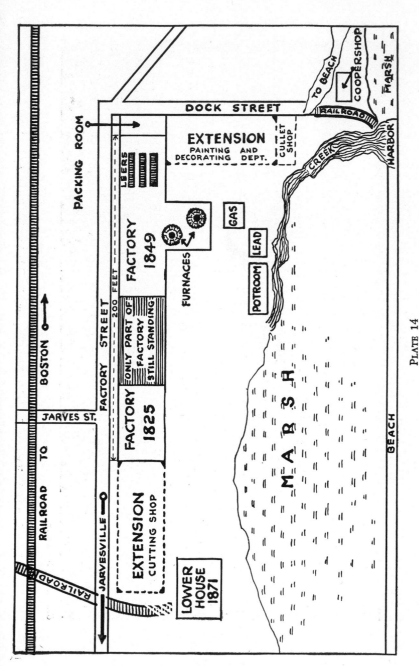

PLATE 14

A general outline showing the gradual development and growth of the Boston & Sandwich Glass Company. The original factory (1825) was absorbed into the main building in the process of expansion.

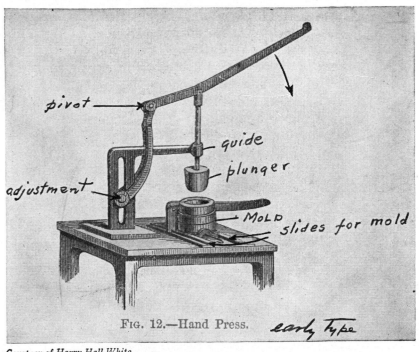

pivot

guide

plunger

adjustment

MOLD

slides for mold

early Type

Fig. 12.—Hand Press.

PLATE 15

Early type of hand press for pressing glass.

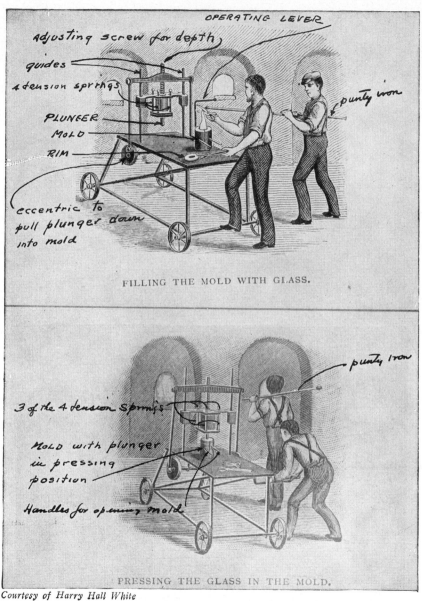

FILLING THE MOLD WITH GLASS.

PRESSING THE GLASS IN THE MOLD.

Courtesy of Harry Hall White

PLATE 16
Early method of pressing glass.

PLATE 17
Side and base view of the first pressed glass tumbler,
made at Sandwich in 1827.

PLATE 18

Glass knobs were among the earliest articles made.

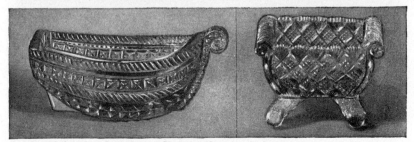

PLATE 19

Top row—Early curtain tie-backs with pewter stems.
Center row—Threaded glass.   *Lower row*—Two early salts

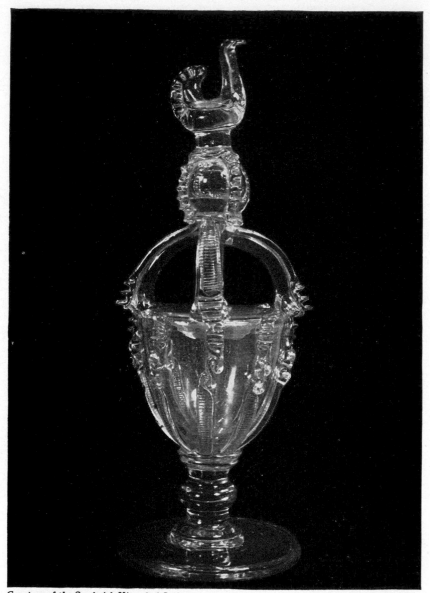

PLATE 20

The rarest example of blown Sandwich glass. A bank, with rooster ornament
and enclosed coin dated 1831.

PLATE 21

Early bird drinking font, with rooster decoration.

PLATE 22—CHALICE

A presentation piece blown and engraved at Sandwich for Deming Jarves' son,
John W. Jarves.

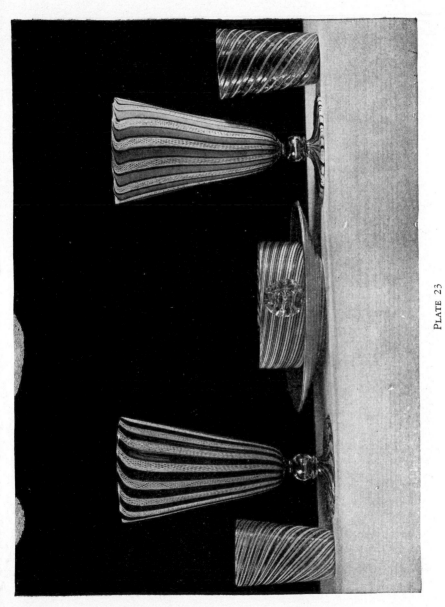

PLATE 23

Authenticated Sandwich "striped" glass, the work of Nicholas Lutz.

PLATE 24
Engraved presentation piece, for Sarah Fuller.

PLATE 25

A window of Threaded glass. Sandwich Historical Society Building.

Collection of the author

PLATE 26

MOLDED SALT DISHES OF THE EARLY 1820's

These were all produced from full-size molds and the rims ground smooth.

PLATE 27

Rare miniature pieces, all of Sandwich origin, with the possible exception of the creamer at the right, which is an unique specimen.

PLATE 28

Miniature decanters and cordial glasses, with corresponding Sandwich fragments.

PLATE 29

Footed salt with Diamond Sunburst and Chevron pattern together with Blown Molded fragments excavated at Sandwich.

PLATE 30

Upper—Quarter-pint decanters.
Lower—Footed salts and hat in familiar patterns.

PLATE 31
Blown Molded caster bottles and salts.

PLATE 32

Tumbler and hat, made from the same mold in the rare Bull's Eye Sunburst. Clear glass inkwell, with Diamond Sunburst.

PLATE 33   BLOWN MOLDED GLASS

PLATE 34—BLOWN MOLDED GLASS IN COLOR
Examples of pitchers, salts and a hat, all rare in sapphire blue.

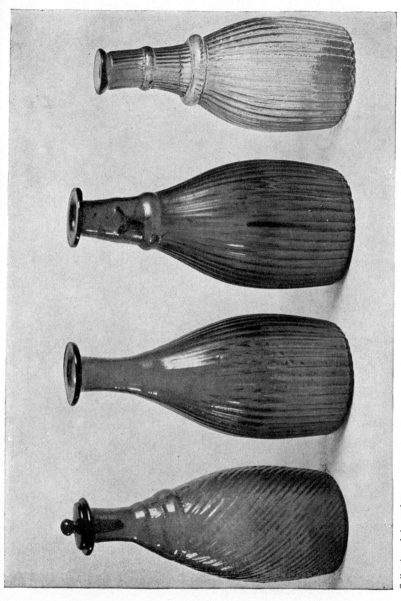

PLATE 35

Group of Blown Molded Vinegar bottles in varying shades of blue.

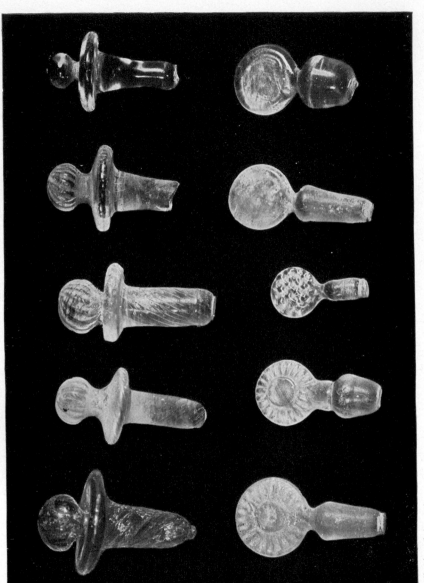

PLATE 36

Examples of early types of stoppers, found in excavations at Sandwich.

PLATE 37

Diamond quilted sugar bowls, the lower with band of diagonal ribbing.

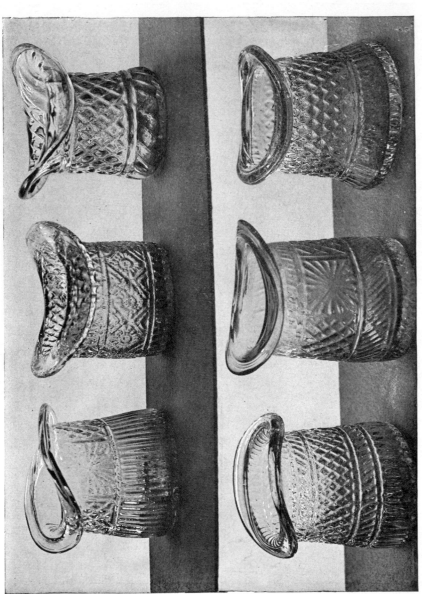

PLATE 38

Blown Molded hats were made in many, though not in all, of the patterns used on other objects.
Period 1828-1840.

PLATE 39

Rare wines and cordial glasses. The misshapen one in the center may well be among the earliest produced.

PLATE 40

Early tumblers, tall wines and a mustard bottle.

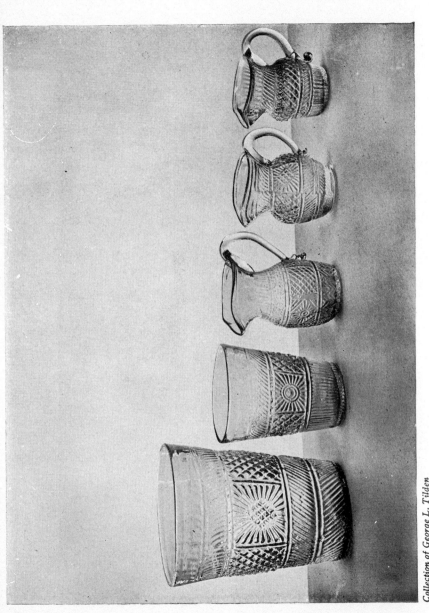

PLATE 41—BLOWN MOLDED FLIP GLASSES AND CREAMERS

Left to right: Patterns 1, Diamond Quilted Sunburst; 2, Double-ringed Bull's Eye Sunburst; 3, Diamond Sunburst; 4, Diamond Quilted Sunburst; 5, Diamond quilting with diagonal ribbing.

PLATE 42

Two Blown Molded flip glasses, half-pint decanter and tumbler, all in the same pattern.

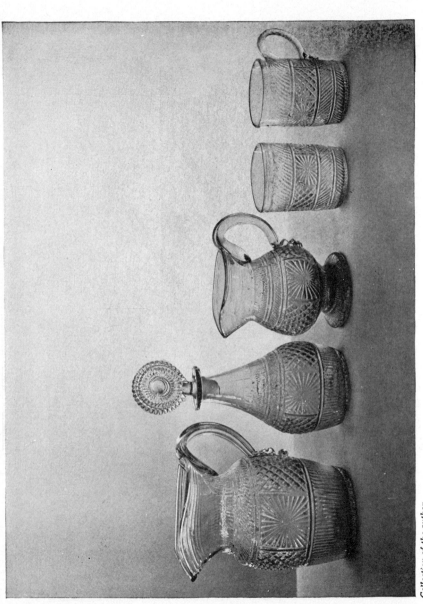

PLATE 43—SUNBURST MOTIF IN BLOWN MOLDED GLASS

Left to right—Pint pitcher, half-pint decanter, creamer, whiskey tumbler, handled mug.

PLATE 44

Diamond quilted pint decanters, flip glass and half-pint pitcher.

PLATE 45

Unidentified Blown Molded syrup jugs.

PLATE 46

Upper—Baroque quart pitcher, Chain with Heart.
Lower—Quart decanter, Chain pattern.   Pint pitcher, Beaded Arch.

PLATE 47—BLOWN MOLDED QUART DECANTERS
Star pattern.   Chain with Heart.

PLATE 48

Fragments of decanters and stoppers excavated at Sandwich.   Period 1830-1840.

PLATE 49

Complete decanters corresponding to fragments shown in preceding illustration.

PLATE 50

Unidentified Blown Molded decanters, which may be of Sandwich origin.

PLATE 51—QUART DECANTERS

Left to right—1, Waffle Sunburst; 2, Diamond Sunburst; 3, Concentric ring Sunburst; 4, Diamond quilted Band.

PLATE 52

Quart Blown Molded decanter in a rare ribbed pattern.

PLATE 53—DIAMOND QUILTED BOWLS, WITH SUNBURST MOTIFS

Sizes: 7⅜ inches   10 inches   8⅜ inches

PLATE 54

Rare examples of a Blown Molded celery vase, sugar bowl and an inkwell with Sunburst motif.

PLATE 55

Rare diamond quilted celery vase of a type made at Sandwich; period 1828-1840.
Design possibly copied from Irish (Cork) "Diamond Cutting and Flutes Celery Glass."

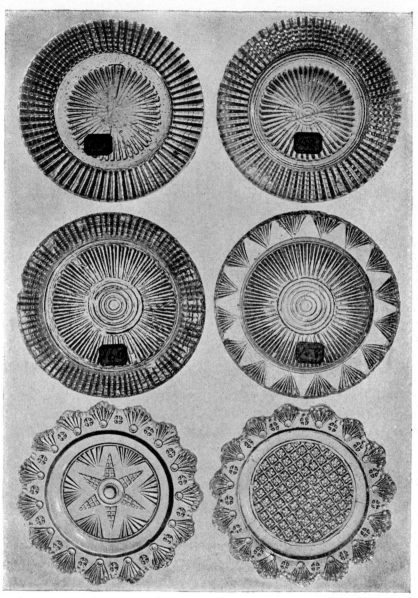

PLATE 56
Evolution of design at Sandwich. Period 1827-1830.

PLATE 57

Five of the ten rarest Historical cup plates, largely Midwestern.

PLATE 58
Five of the ten rarest Historical cup plates from New England and the Midwest.

PLATE 59
Five of the eleven rarest Conventional cup plates from New England and the Midwest.

PLATE 60
Six of the eleven rarest Conventional cup plates, largely Midwestern.

PLATE 61—"GLASSED-IN PASTES"

Not cup plates but made in various European countries for use as ornaments, suspended from the wall.

PLATE 62

Bust of Napoleon.   Plate probably made in France by "glassed-in paste" process patented by Apsley Pellatt in England.

PLATE 63

Authenticated Sandwich cup plates with corresponding fragments and additional pieces taken from the site of the old factory. Period 1827-1835.

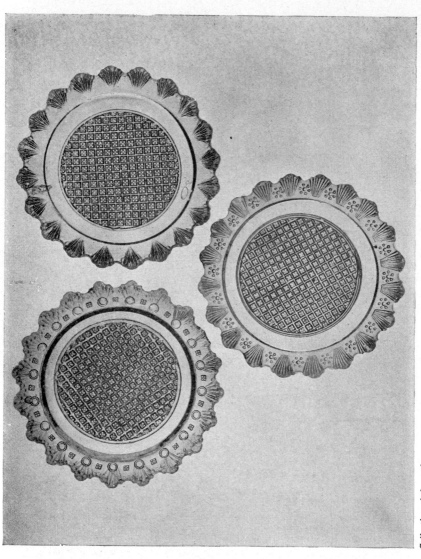

PLATE 64

Early pressed plates (7 inch) which preceded those with stippled backgrounds, circa 1828.

PLATE 65

Large bowl (10¾ inches) of the Heart series, circa 1830.

PLATE 66
Large bowl (9½ inches) of the Heart series, circa 1830.

PLATE 67
Unusually large, heavy bowl, circa 1830.

PLATE 68

Fragments of lacy Sandwich glass, found in excavations under building erected in 1849.

PLATE 69
Group of salts, including three rare types with covers.

PLATE 70
Early salts, including the rare Washington-Lafayette.

PLATE 71
Group of early salts.

PLATE 72—FIVE MARKED SALTS

Upper—"Sandwich, Lafayet."   Side view and marked interior.
Center—"Jersey Glass Co."; Locomotive "H. Clay."
Lower—"Providence"; "N. E. Glass Company, Boston."

PLATE 73
Lacy salts in color.

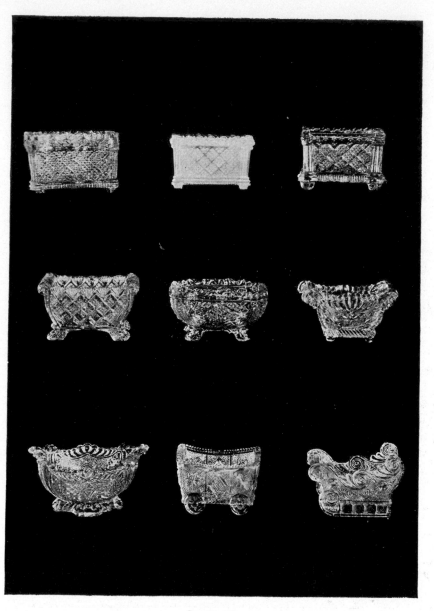

PLATE 74
Group of choice lacy salts.

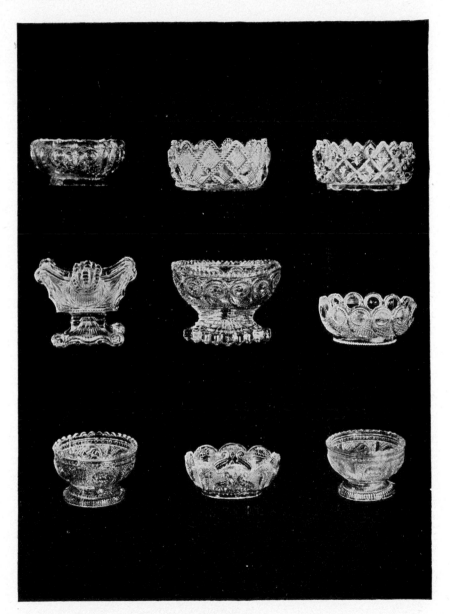

PLATE 75
Group of choice salts, including the two variants of the rare Cadmus-Eagle.

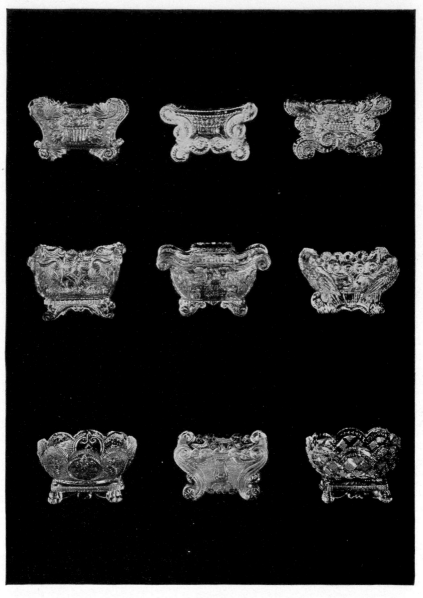

PLATE 76
Rare lacy salts.

PLATE 77
Lacy salts.

PLATE 78
Lacy salts.

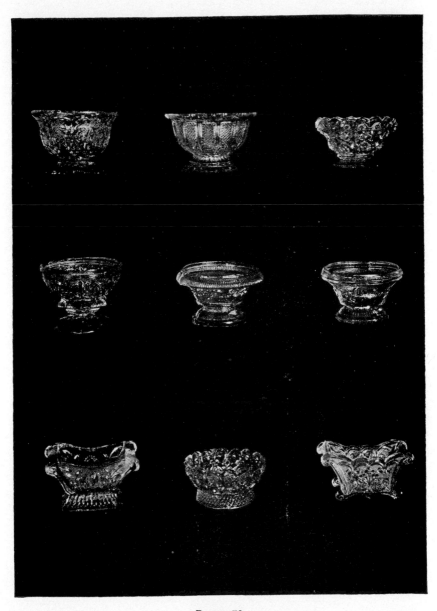

PLATE 79
Lacy salts.

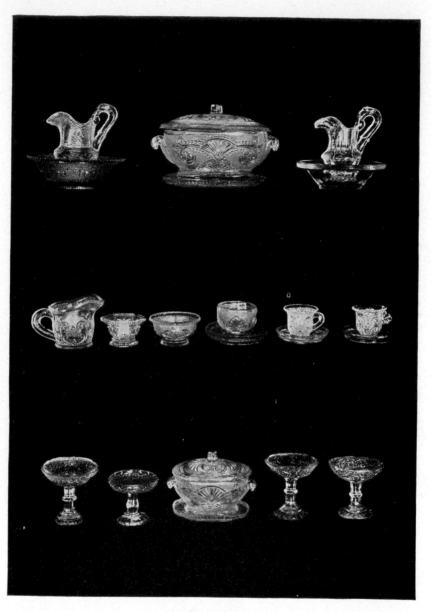

PLATE 80
Miniature lacy pieces.

PLATE 81
Miniature lacy pieces. Oval dish at upper right is Midwestern.

PLATE 82

Upper: Miniature rectangular footed dishes, side view and center of bowl.
Lower: Opaque blue miniature plate and three others in clear glass, the one in lower
right being Midwestern.

PLATE 83
Two views of Miniature candlesticks and four plates.

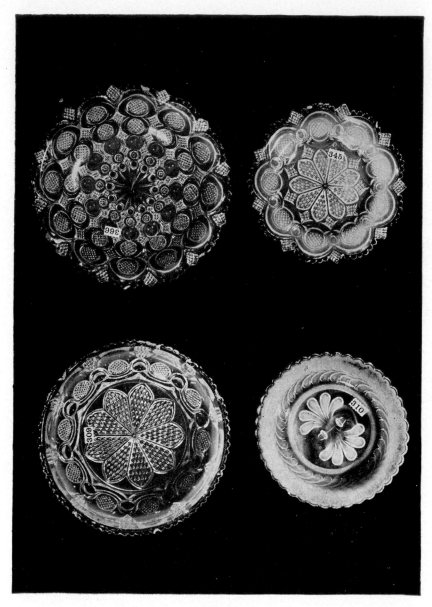

PLATE 84

Early sauce dishes and small bowls.
Upper—Stippled Bull's Eye; Roman Rosette.
Lower—Diamond Rosette; Plume.

PLATE 85—SAUCE DISHES

Left to right. *Upper*—Crossed Swords. Rayed Peacock Eye.
Center—Nectarine. Oak Leaf.
Lower—Peacock Eye. Double leaf.

PLATE 86—LARGE SAUCE DISHES

Left to right. *Upper*—5 inch plate, Crown in center. 5¼ inch, Thistle.
Center—5¼ inch, Nectarine. 5 inch, Gothic Arch.
Lower—5½ inch, Rayed Peacock Eye. 6 inch, Shell Medallion.

PLATE 87—LARGE SAUCE DISHES

Upper—Crossed Swords, 5⅜ inches.   Shell pattern, 5½ inches.
Lower—Star Medallion, 6 inches.   Nectarine, 5½ inches.

PLATE 88

Small sauce dishes, found frequently in color.

Plume and Diamond   Panelled Scroll

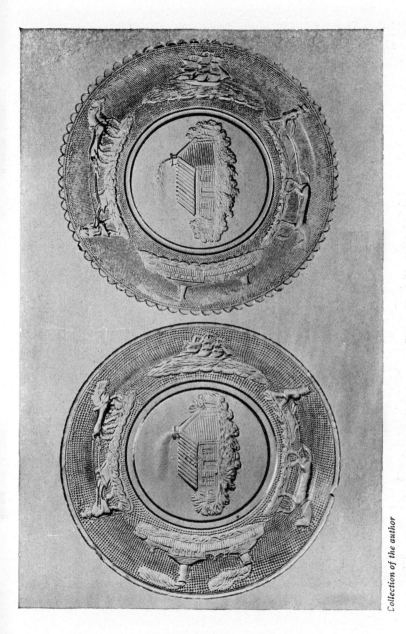

PLATE 89

Two examples of the log cabin, "Industry" bowls.

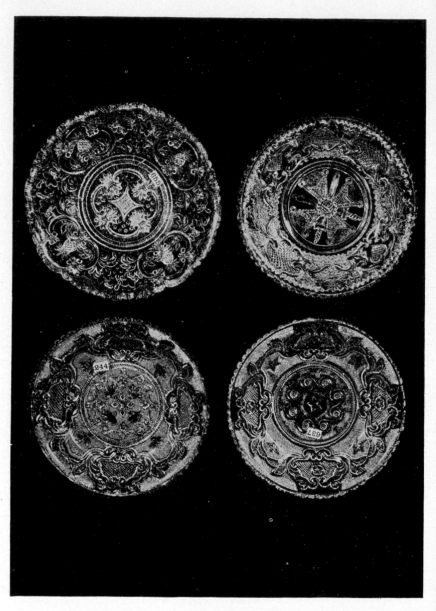

PLATE 90
Three bowls with variations of the Princess Feather medallion.
Upper left, early Pineapple design.

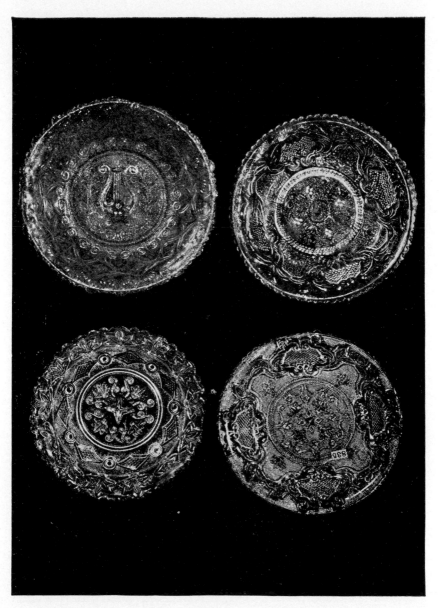

PLATE 91
Four early small bowls. Two employ Princess Feather medallions.

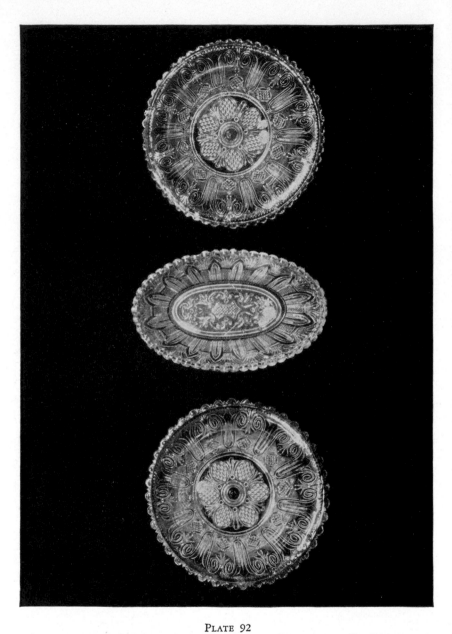

PLATE 92

Two 7½ inch bowls with different edge serrations. Oval deep dish. Top bowl and lower
one are of late Midwestern origin.

PLATE 93

Four lacy 7½ inch bowls. Three are in the Nectarine pattern and the fourth is Oak Leaf.

PLATE 94
Four choice 8 inch lacy bowls.

PLATE 95

Butterfly trays and a variant.

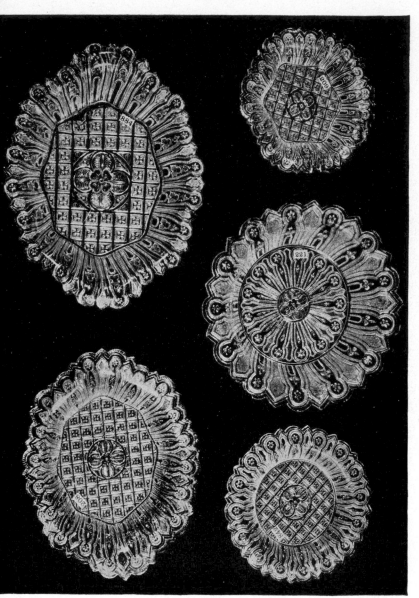

PLATE 96—A GROUP OF RARE DISHES IN THE HAIRPIN PATTERN

Upper—Oval deep dish, 8⅝ x 6¾ inches. Large oval, 10 x 7½ inches.

Lower—Plate, 6 inches. Large round deep bowl, 8 x 1½ inches deep. Hexagonal dish, 5½ inches.

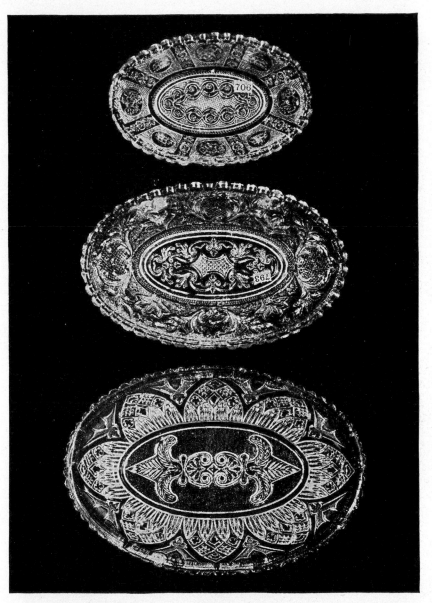

PLATE 97
Oval deep dishes, including the Cadmus-Eagle.

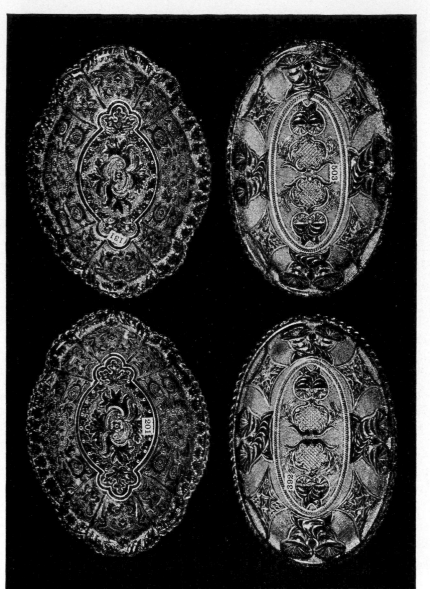

PLATE 98

Two pairs of rare oval dishes.

PLATE 99
Rare large oval deep dishes.

PLATE 100
Oblong shallow tray.

PLATE 101
Gothic oblong dishes in three sizes.

PLATE 102
Small and large oblong deep dishes. All except center row are of Midwestern origin.

PLATE 103
Large oblong deep dishes. The largest is Midwestern.

PLATE 104
Early 5¾ and 6 inch plates.

PLATE 105
Heart variants, in 5 and 6 inch sizes.

PLATE 106
Early plates. Period 1828–1840. Three belong to the Heart Series.
The fourth is the Plaid pattern.

PLATE 107
Three Heart variants. Odd plate, upper left, attributed to the Midwest.

PLATE 108
Four early opaque white plates. Period 1830-1840.

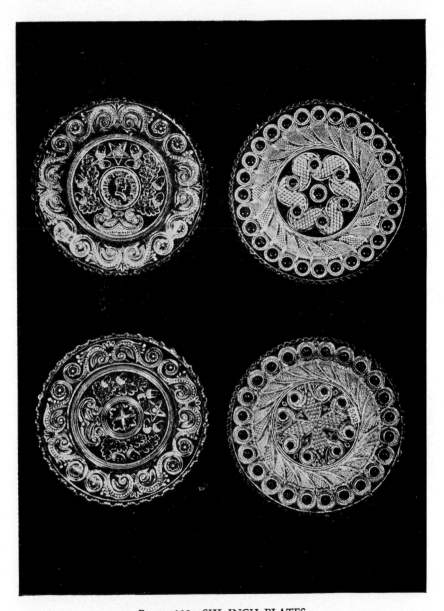

PLATE 109—SIX INCH PLATES

Upper—"Washington George" plate.   Peacock Eye plate.
Lower—Variant of above.   Peacock Eye plate.

PLATE 110

Six inch plates. The one at lower left is usually found in Philadelphia area. The lower right is Midwestern.

PLATE 111
Four small plates and two sauce dishes.

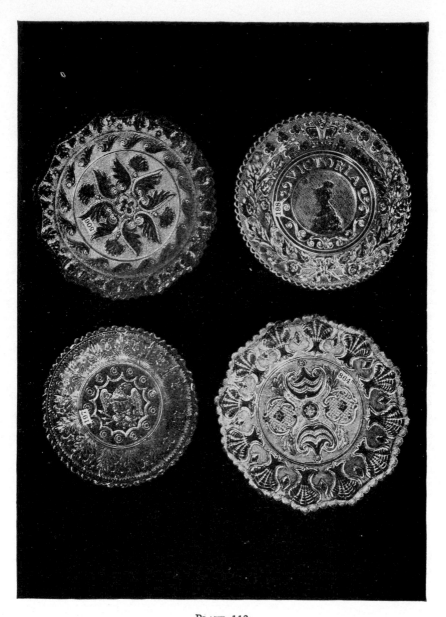

PLATE 112

Four lacy plates, including a rare "Victoria" and an "Eagle." The Eagle plate is Midwestern.

PLATE 113
Four early lacy plates.

PLATE 114

Upper—Peacock Eye mustard cup with cover. Sauce plate of same pattern but not
designed to use with cup.
Lower—Peacock Eye and Thistle plate.

PLATE 115—EACH FROM A DIFFERENT FACTORY

Top—Sandwich, Rayed Peacock Eye.
Left—French, probably Baccarat.
Right—Midwestern.

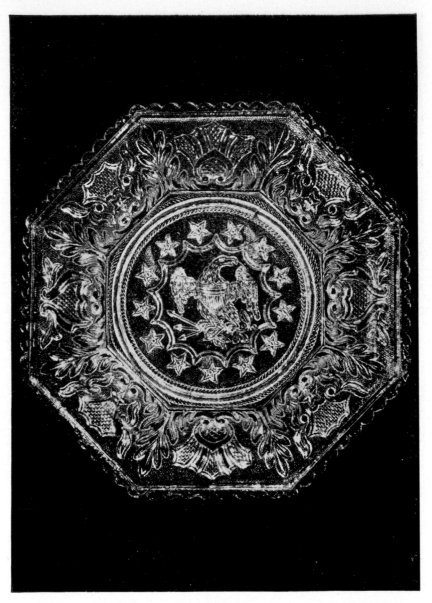

PLATE 116
Rare octagonal plate with eagle and thirteen stars.

PLATE 117
Extremely rare 12 inch bowl.
Princess Feather medallions alternate with **Peacock Eye** motif. Period 1830–1840.

PLATE 118
Rare 11 inch lacy bowl. Trefoil with circular medallion.

PLATE 119
Rare 10 inch bowl. Princess Feather medallion with diamond motif.

PLATE 120
Rare 9 inch bowl. Fleur-de-lys and Thistle pattern.

PLATE 121
Rare 10 inch bowl, Dahlia pattern.

PLATE 122
Acanthus Leaf 9¼ inch bowl.

PLATE 123
Rare 10 inch deep dish, Feather pattern.

PLATE 124
Feather 9½ inch deep dish with quatrefoil center.

PLATE 125

Deep bowl and a 9½ inch plate, in Feather with quatrefoil center.

PLATE 126

Oak Leaf 9¼ inch shallow bowl.

PLATE 127
Oak Leaf shallow bowl.

PLATE 128
Oak Leaf bowl with beaded border.

PLATE 129
Gothic Arch 9½ inch bowl.

PLATE 130
Daisy 9 inch bowl.

PLATE 131
Two large Tulip and Acanthus Leaf bowls, with edge variations.

PLATE 132
Two large Peacock Eye bowls.

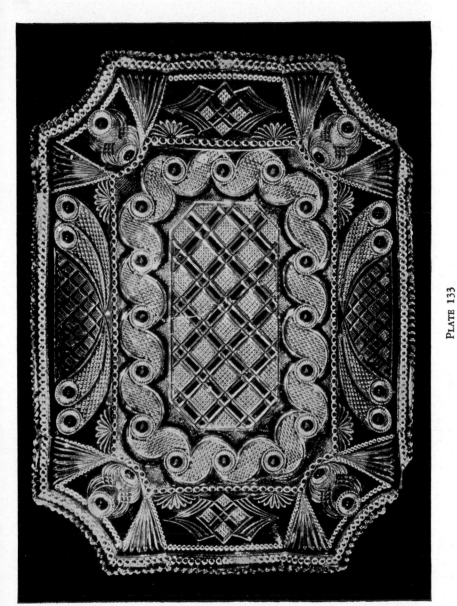

PLATE 133

Large oblong vegetable dish, in Peacock Eye.

PLATE 134

Upper—Cobalt Blue Daisy with Peacock Eye border.
Lower—Large Shield with Fleur-de-lys bowl.

PLATE 135
Princess Feather 8½ inch bowl.

PLATE 136—OCTAGONAL CAKE PLATES

Upper—Beehive 9¼ inch plate.
Lower—Rose and Thistle 8¾ inch plate.

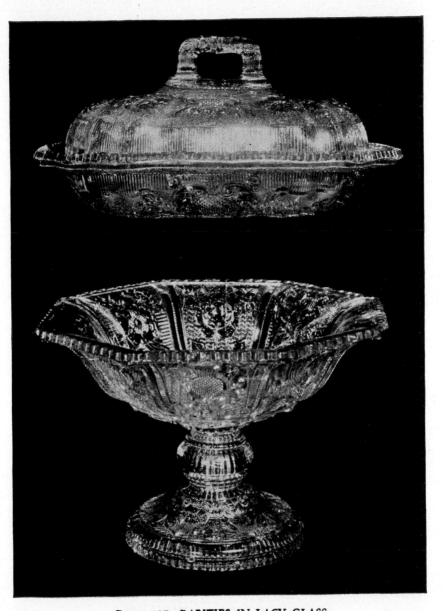

PLATE 137—RARITIES IN LACY GLASS

Upper—Large covered vegetable dish.
Lower—Octagonal compote with flowered panels.

PLATE 138—RARITIES IN LACY GLASS

Upper—Peacock Eye butter dish.
Lower—Exceptionally large Peacock Eye compote, 10½ inch.

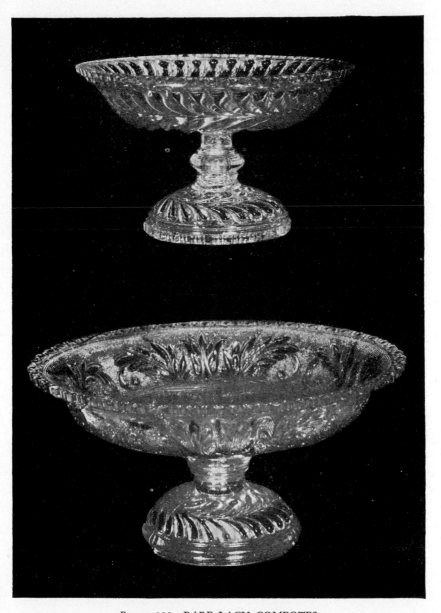

PLATE 139—RARE LACY COMPOTES
Upper—Plume pattern.
Lower—Tulip bowl, Plume pedestal, all original.

PLATE 140
Rare Dahlia compote. Scrolled pedestal with triangular base and paw feet.

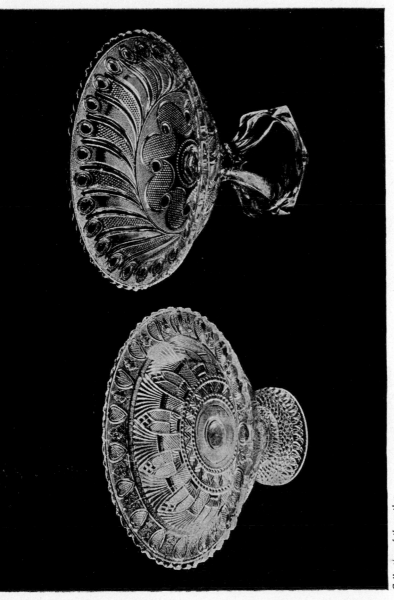

PLATE 141

Rare large Heart with Leaf compote.   The Peacock Eye in an unusual combination with a clear, hexagonal foot.

PLATE 142

Rare large oblong Peacock Eye compote with interesting scrolled pedestal
and round foot.

PLATE 143
Rayed Peacock Eye compotes with differing pedestals,

PLATE 144
Four interesting types of lacy compotes. The one at the upper right is Midwestern.

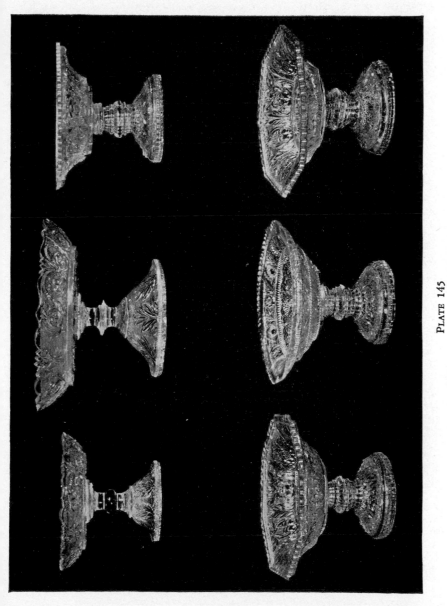

PLATE 145

A group of rare lacy compotes, including a pair in the Nectarine pattern.

PLATE 146
Compotes in the Nectarine pattern.

PLATE 147
Rare compote found in blue, amethyst or yellow, as well as clear glass.

PLATE 148

Two Peacock Eye and two Paneled Diamond compotes.

PLATE 149
Two lacy Princess Feather compotes.

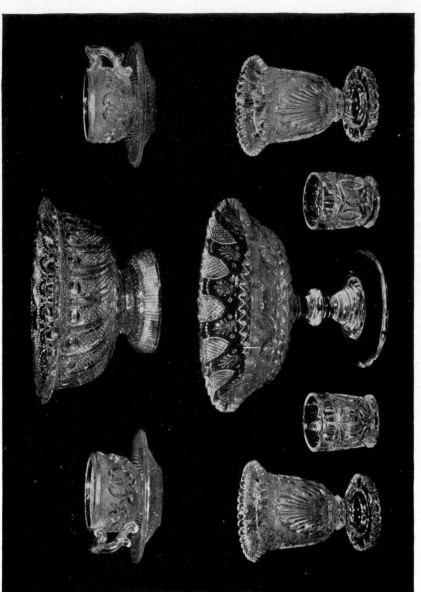

PLATE 150—GROUP OF LACY DISHES

Upper—Pair of lacy cups and saucers. Peacock Eye footed bowl.
Lower—Pair of lacy egg glasses. Heart with Sheaf of Wheat compote. Pair of whiskey tasters.

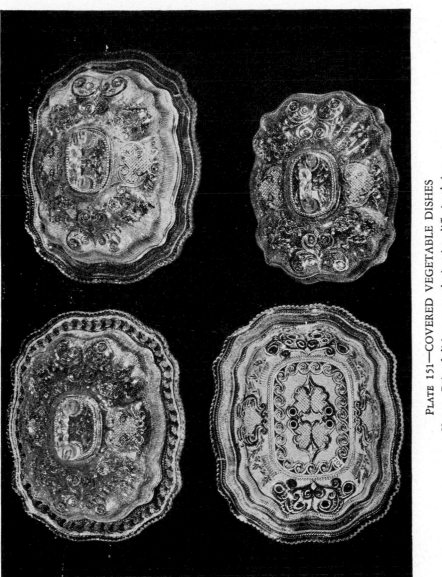

PLATE 151—COVERED VEGETABLE DISHES

Upper—Pair of dishes, covered, showing differing brims.
Lower—Base to dish, with cover at one side.

PLATE 152

Porcelain dish bearing Meissen mark of the 1820's, from which design on vegetable dish with grape border on Plate 151 was apparently copied.

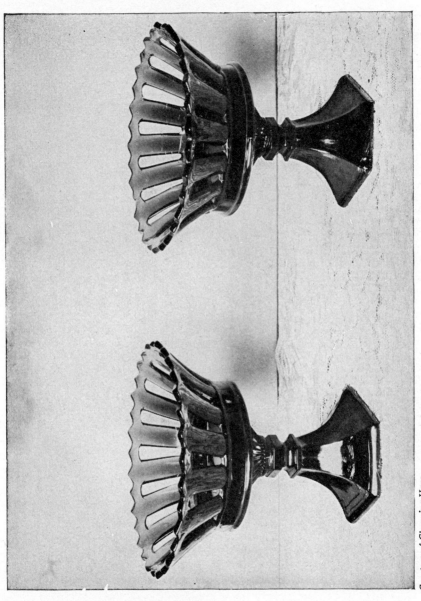

PLATE 153

Pair of extremely rare amethyst compotes.

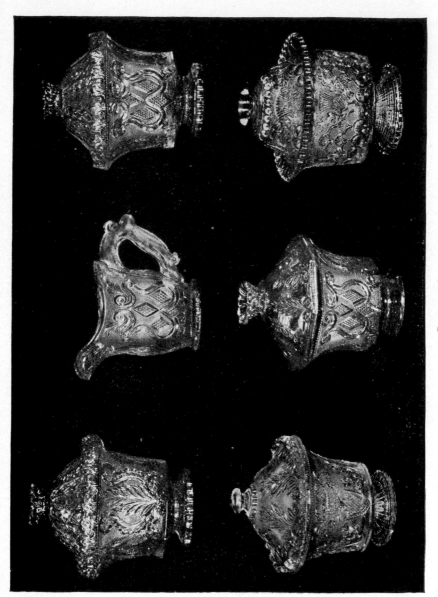

PLATE 154

Rare lacy sugar bowls and creamer.

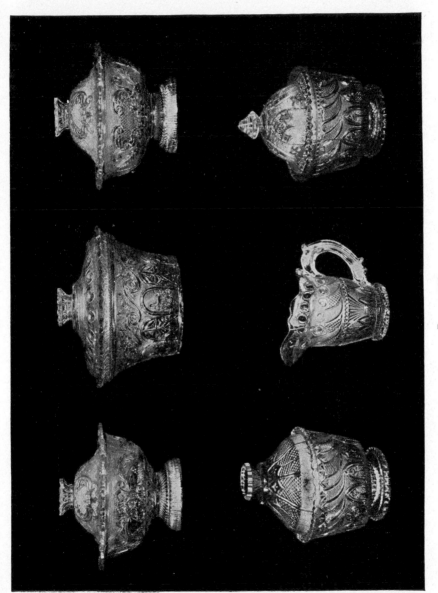

PLATE 155

Rare lacy covered bowls and creamer.

PLATE 156
Rare colored sugar bowls and creamer. Lower left bowl is Midwestern.

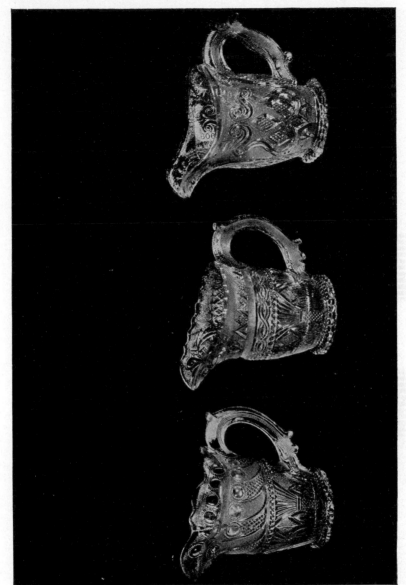

PLATE 157
Lacy creamers.

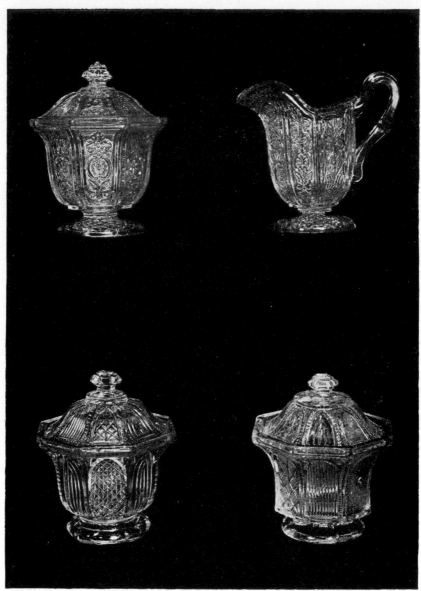

PLATE 158

Upper—Sugar bowl and creamer of later period.
Lower—Two sugar bowls. That on the left not positively identified as Sandwich.

PLATE 159
Creamer marked "R. B. Curling & Sons, Fort Pitt."
The Fort Pitt Glass Works was located in Pittsburgh, Pa.

PLATE 160

Lacy pane of Pittsburgh origin, marked "Curling's & Robertson." This was made by the Fort Pitt Glass Works.

PLATE 161

Upper: Lacy glass pane, unmarked, found in Pittsburgh.
Lower left: Lacy pane, found in Ohio. Lower right: Small view of marked pane.

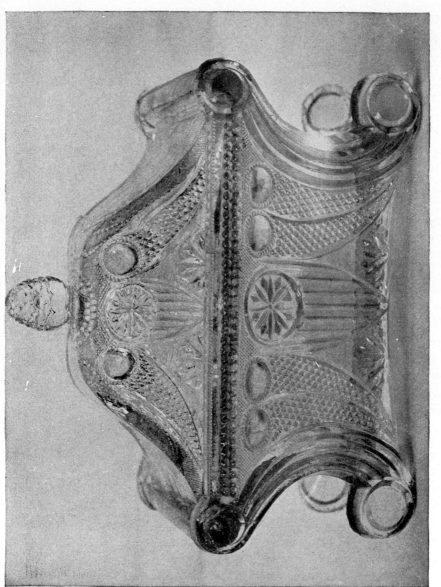

PLATE 162

Extremely rare lacy jewel casket.

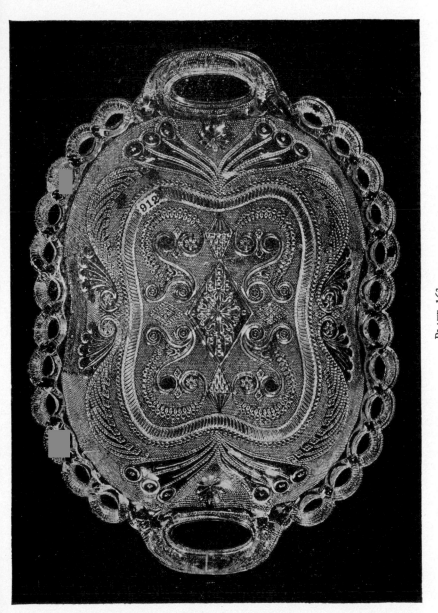

PLATE 163

Extremely rare deep dish with open chain border. Size 11½ x 8 inches.

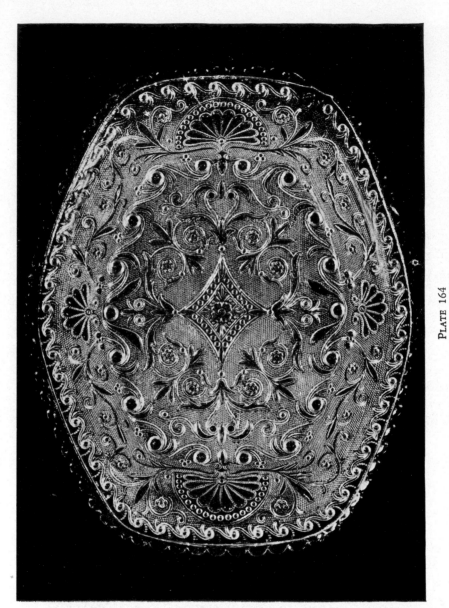

PLATE 164

Extremely rare large shallow tray. One of the most beautiful of all the lacy designs. Size 10¾ by 9 inches.

PLATE 165

Rare deep vegetable dish. Size 10 x 8½ inches.

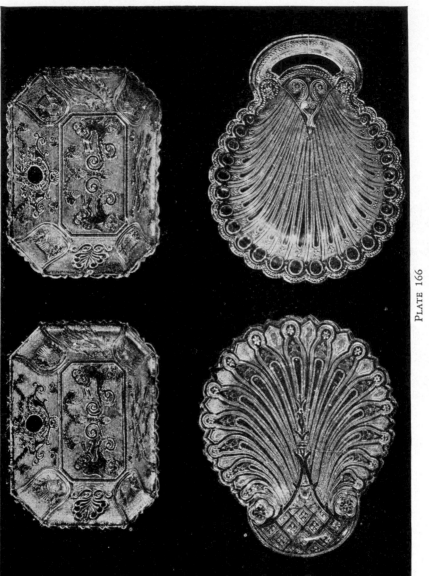

PLATE 166

Upper—Pair of Pipes of Pan oblong dishes.
Lower—Two large shell-shaped dishes.

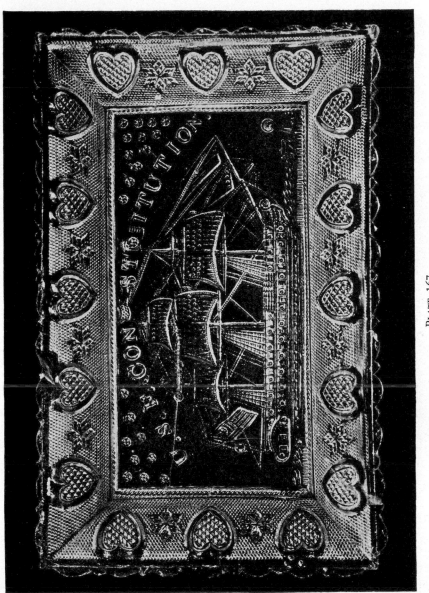

Plate 167

Rare oblong tray showing "U. S. Frigate Constitution."

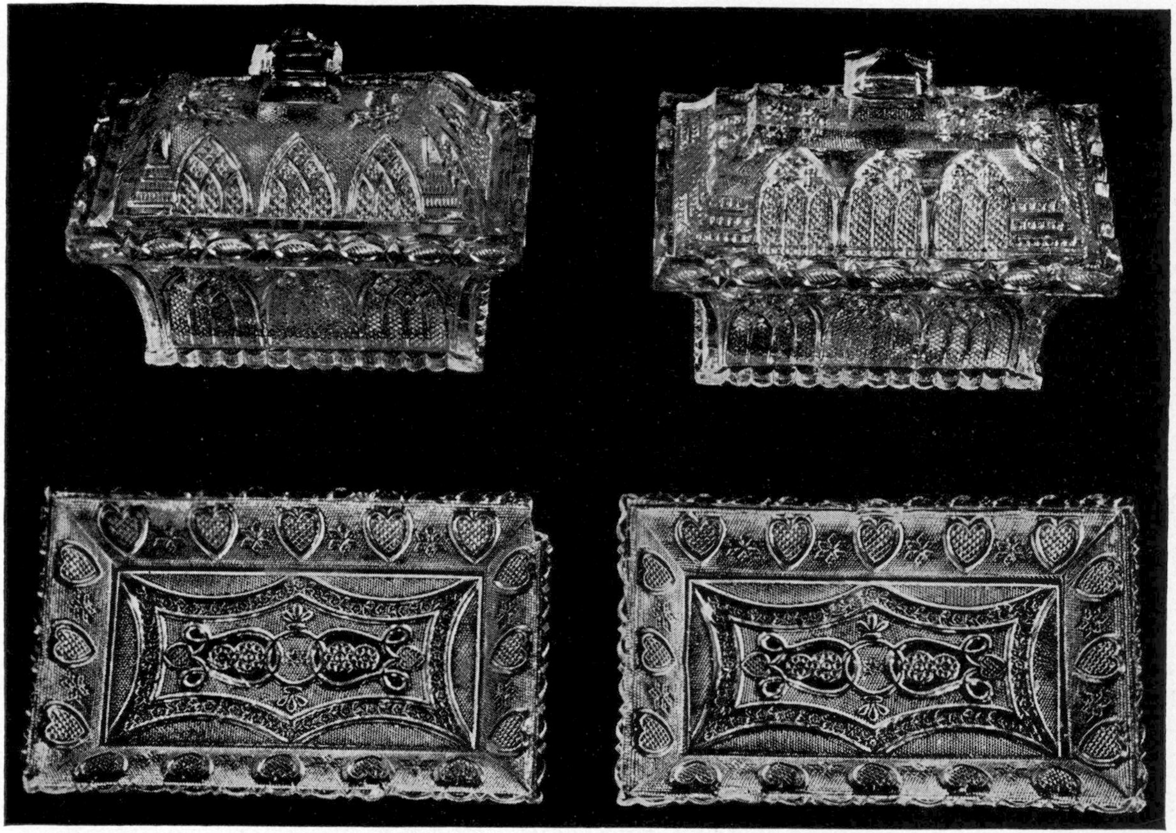

PLATE 168

Covered oblong deep dishes and trays.

PLATE 169

Group of 6 inch plates, attributed to Midwestern glass district.

PLATE 170

Group of 5 inch plates and oblong tray. Unidentified factory; attributed to Midwest.

PLATE 171
Group of Baccarat and other French lacy pieces.

PLATE 172
French lacy glass, circa 1840.

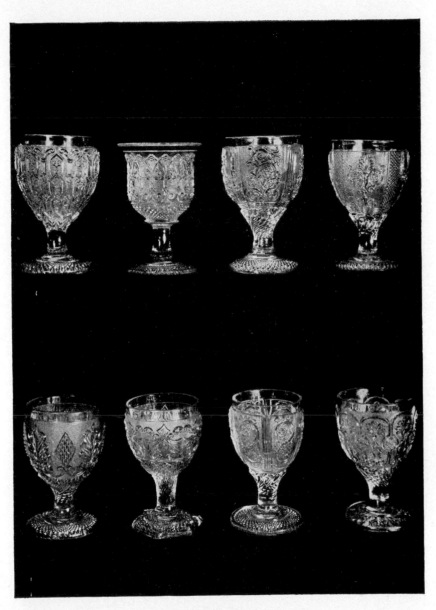

PLATE 173
French lacy goblets, circa 1840.

PLATE 174

French lacy glass, circa 1840.

PLATE 175
Baccarat. Period 1840-1860.

PLATE 176
Large bowls of European origin.

PLATE 177
Early, rare lacy candlesticks. Period 1830-1835.

PLATE 178
Early lamp and group of candlesticks. Period 1830-1835.

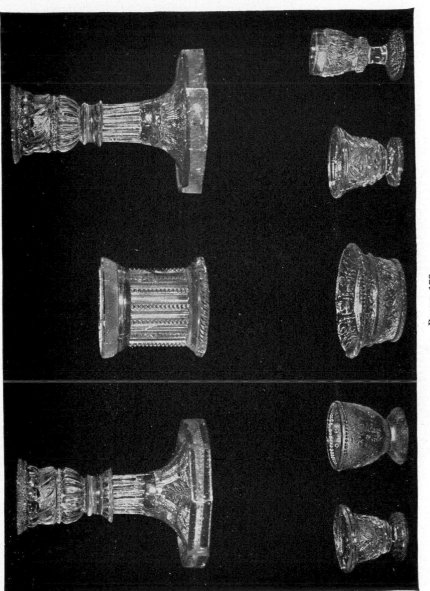

PLATE 179

Upper—Choice pair of lacy candlesticks and sandshaker.
Lower—Group of miscellaneous salts and a cordial glass.

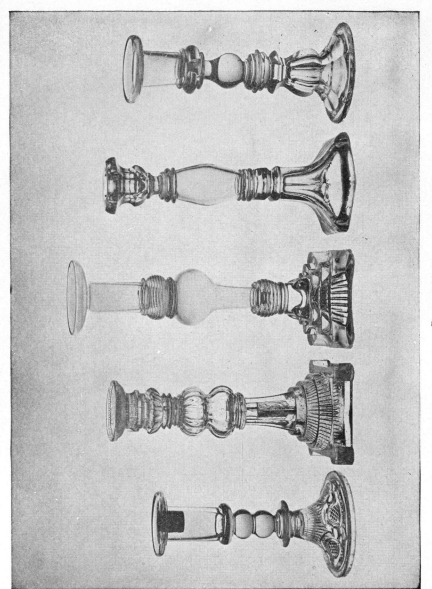

PLATE 180

Early candlesticks, blown and pressed.   Period 1830-1835.

PLATE 181

Early candlesticks. Period 1830-1835.

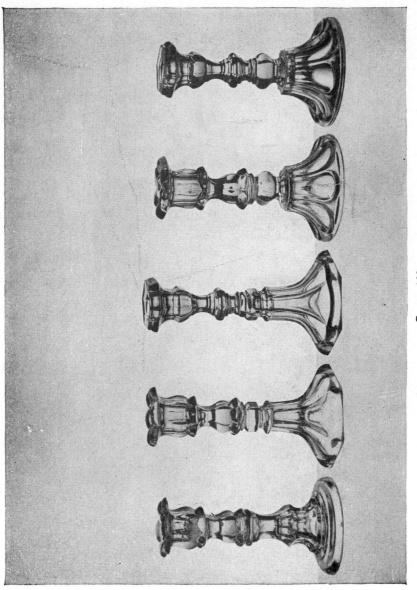

PLATE 182

Early candlesticks. Period 1835-1840.

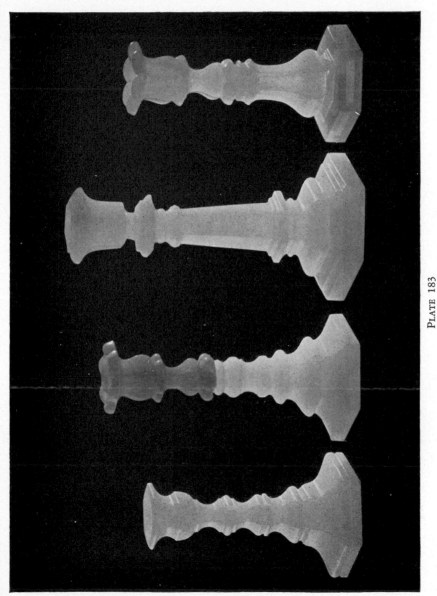

PLATE 183

Opaque candlesticks. Period 1840-1850.

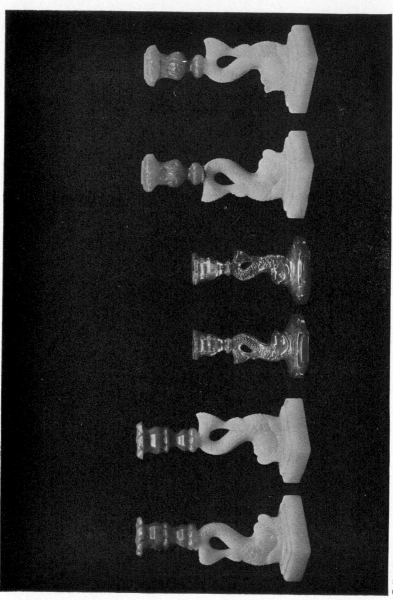

Collection of W. Colston Leigh

PLATE 184

Dolphin candlesticks, circa 1840. The small pair in the center may be Midwestern.

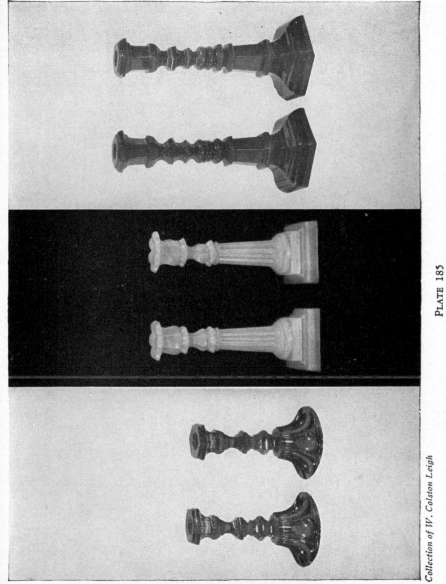

PLATE 185

Three pairs of candlesticks. Period 1830-1840.

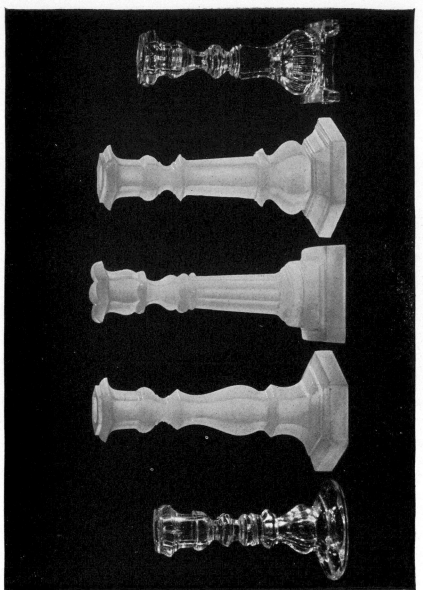

PLATE 186
Early candlesticks, circa 1840.

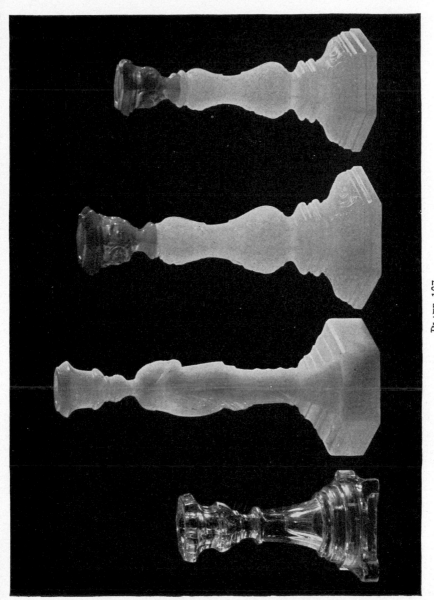

PLATE 187

Group of candlesticks. Period 1840-1850.

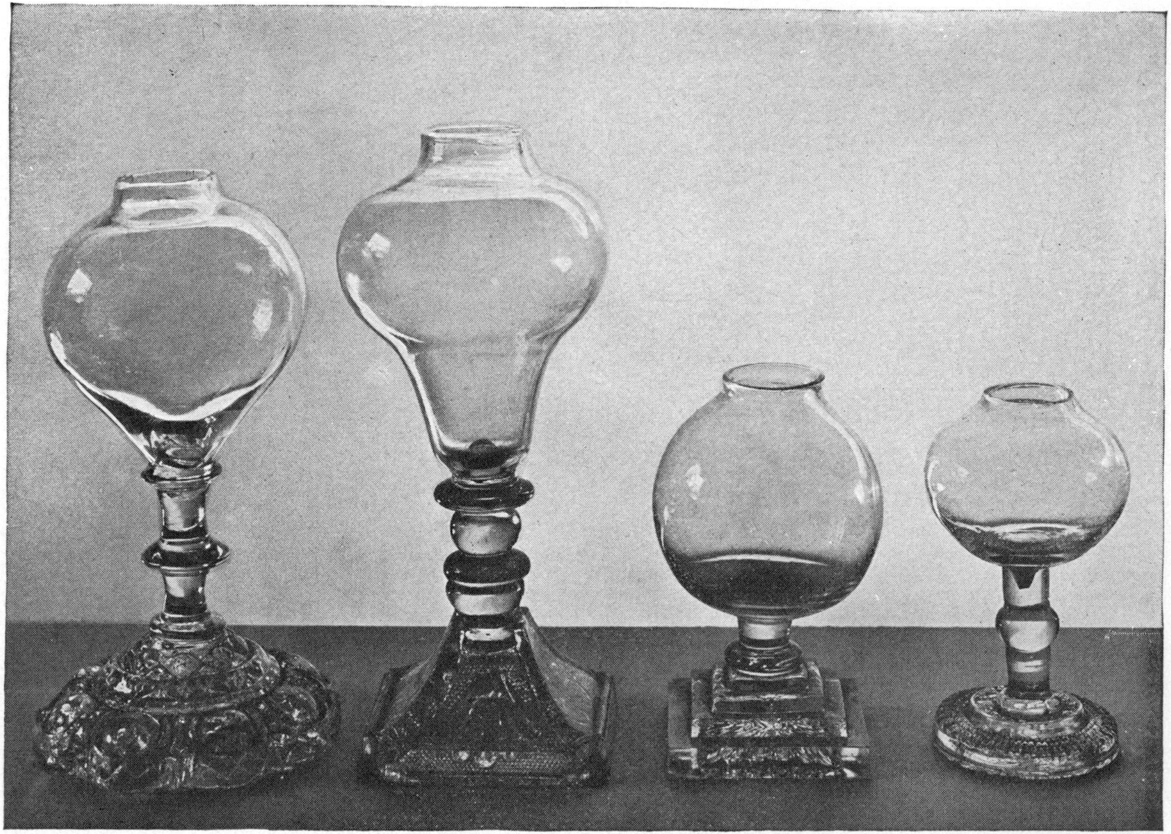

Collection of George L. Tilden

PLATE 188

Early blown and pressed, whale oil lamps.

PLATE 189

Early blown and pressed. whale oil lamps.

Collection of Dorothy White O'Reilly

PLATE 190
Pair of early blown lamps, with pressed lacy foot.

PLATE 191

Pair of large, exceptionally handsome whale oil lamps; blown, cut bowl
and pressed foot.

Collection of George L. Tilden

PLATE 192

Colored glass whale oil lamps. Period 1835-1845.

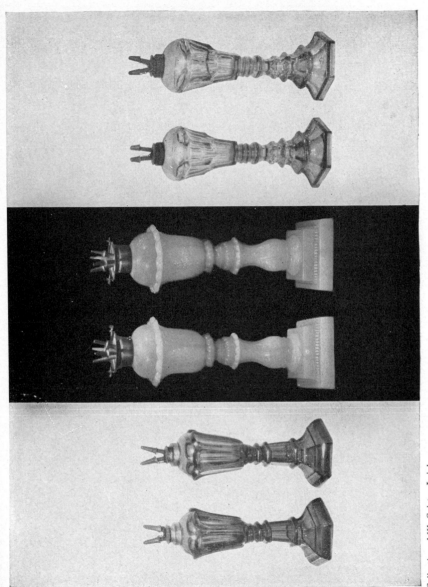

PLATE 193

Three pairs of whale oil lamps. Period 1830-1840.

PLATE 194
Choice overlay lamps.

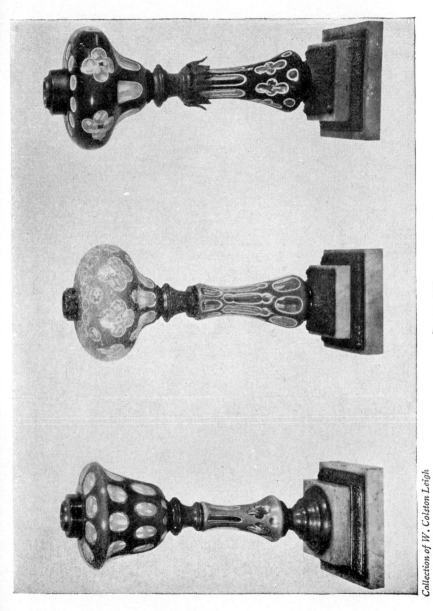

Collection of W. Colston Leigh

PLATE 195

Rare overlay lamps with cut stems. Height 21 inches.

PLATE 196

Rare overlay lamps in a large size. Height 28 inches.

Collection of W. Colston Leigh

PLATE 197
Exceptionally rare overlay lamps. Height 38 inches.

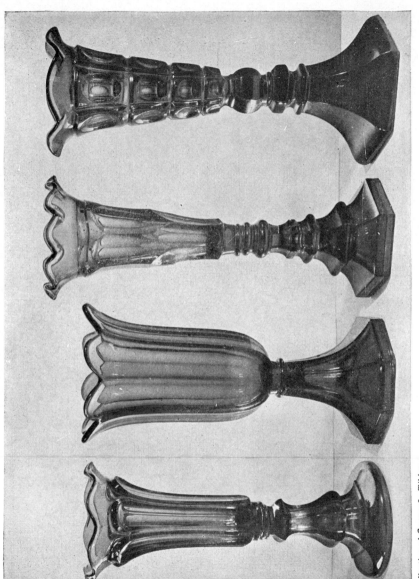

Collection of George L. Tilden

PLATE 198

Sandwich vases in color. Period 1835-1845.

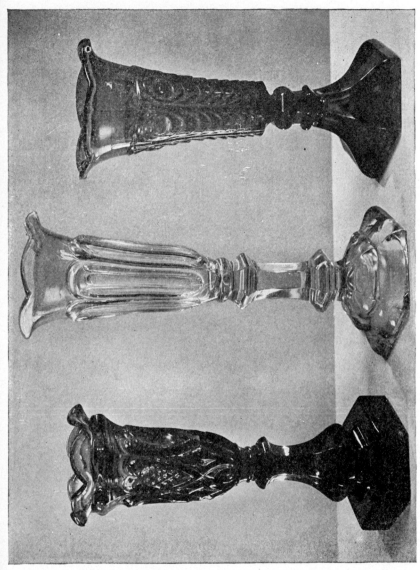

PLATE 199

Sandwich vases in color. Period 1835-1845.

PLATE 200

Sandwich vases in color. Period 1835-1845.

PLATE 201

Sugar bowl and pairs of Sandwich vases in color.

PLATE 202

Six typical paperweights made by Nicholas Lutz at Sandwich.

PLATE 203

FLOWERS AND LEAVES FOR PAPERWEIGHTS

These were all made by Lutz for insertion in his paperweights. Leaf sprays were done with a special hand tool.

PLATE 204

Above: An Apple Paperweight by Lutz, and a flower knob.

Below: Apples, pears, cherries and carrots in various colors, for insertion in weights. Composition bouquets, to be silvered before being encased in paperweights.

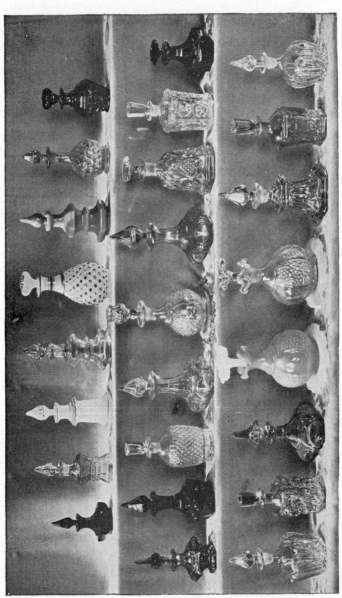

PLATE 205

Group of interesting toilet bottles.

PLATE 206

Group of interesting toiler bottles.

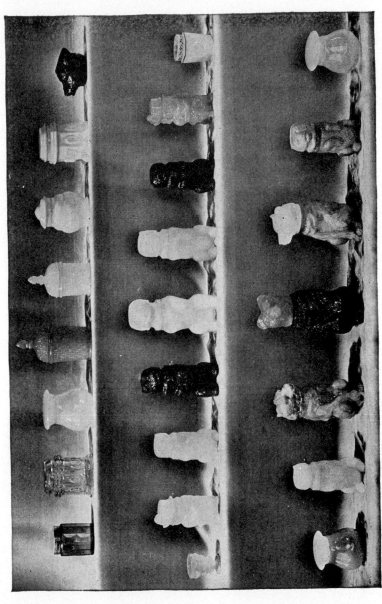

PLATE 207

Bear and "Little Cavalier" ointment jars and other pomade jars.

PLATE 208
Group of interesting early spillholders.

PLATE 209
Upper—Spillholders.
Lower—Smocking pattern

PLATE 210

Upper—Rare oblong Horn of Plenty honey dish.
Lower—Two opaque spillholders and a Cable spoonholder.

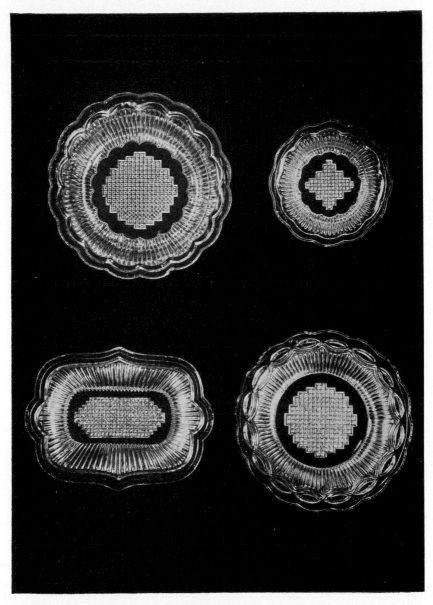

PLATE 211
Group in Rayed, with Loop border.

PLATE 212

Fragments of Diamond patterns excavated at Sandwich.

PLATE 213

Morning Glory goblet, champagne glass and egg cup.

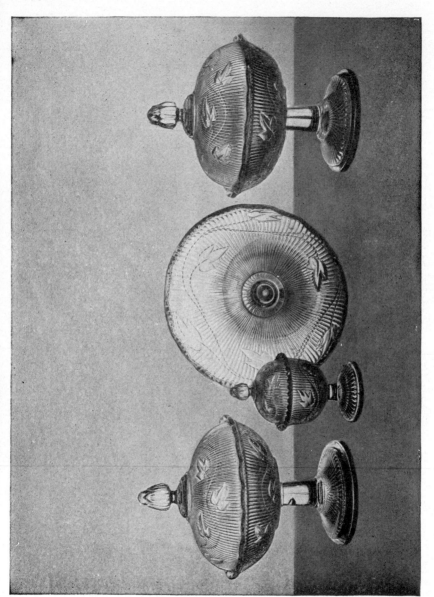

PLATE 214

Group of rarities in the Ivy pattern.

PLATE 215

Tree of Life goblet and footed glass. Sandwich "Overshot" plate and tumbler.

PLATE 216

Upper—Opaque covered egg cups.   Cable; Bull's Eye and Bar.
Lower—Two goblets.   Flat Diamond and Panel; Sandwich Star.

PLATE 217—FOUR AUTHENTICATED SANDWICH PATTERNS

Upper—Bull's Eye and Bar goblet. Flute with Diamond border goblet.
Lower—Beaded Circle goblet. Chrysanthemum Leaf sherbet cup.

PLATE 218—AUTHENTICATED SANDWICH PATTERNS

Upper—Bradford Blackberry; Scalloped Lines; Stippled Fuchsia; Ripple; Dickinson.
Lower—Flowered Oval; Grape Band Variant; Beaded Mirror; Divided Heart; Beaded Acorn.

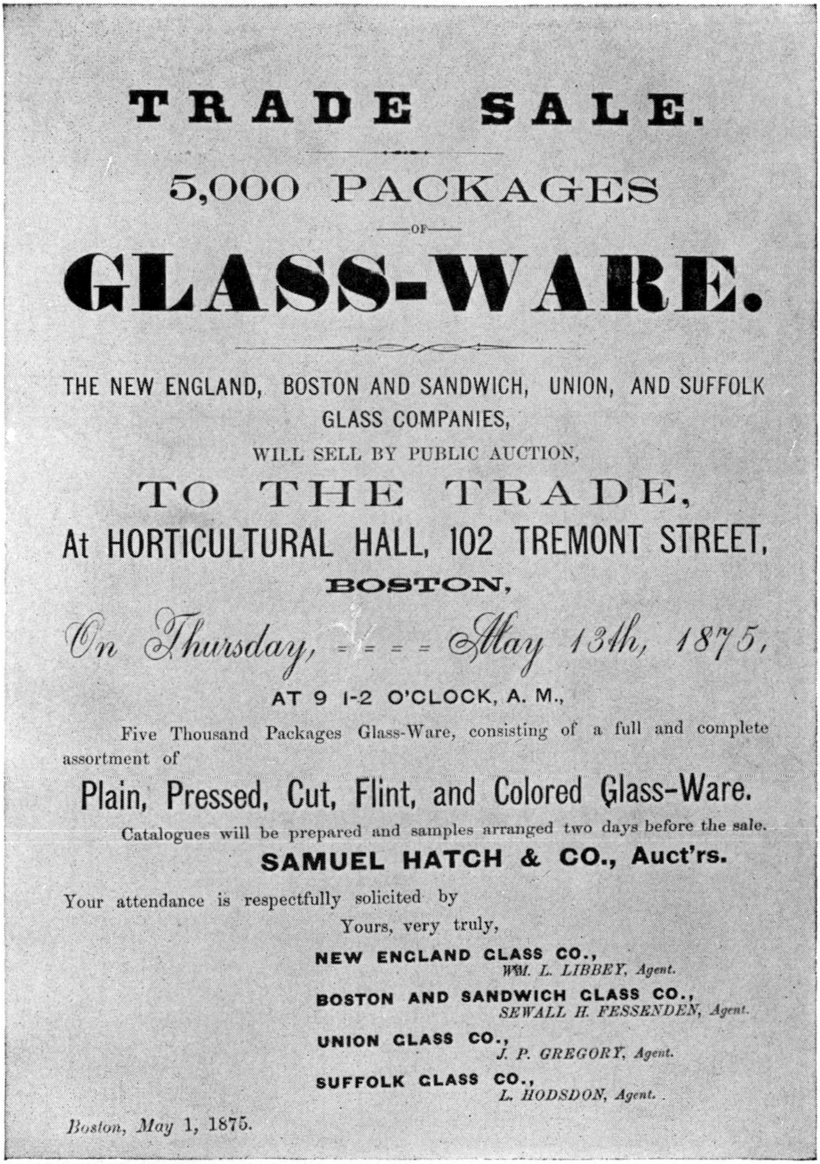

TRADE SALE.

5,000 PACKAGES

—OF—

GLASS-WARE.

THE NEW ENGLAND, BOSTON AND SANDWICH, UNION, AND SUFFOLK GLASS COMPANIES,

WILL SELL BY PUBLIC AUCTION,

TO THE TRADE,

At HORTICULTURAL HALL, 102 TREMONT STREET,

BOSTON,

On Thursday, - - - - May 13th, 1875,

AT 9 1-2 O'CLOCK, A. M.,

Five Thousand Packages Glass-Ware, consisting of a full and complete assortment of

Plain, Pressed, Cut, Flint, and Colored Glass-Ware.

Catalogues will be prepared and samples arranged two days before the sale.

SAMUEL HATCH & CO., Auct'rs.

Your attendance is respectfully solicited by

Yours, very truly,

NEW ENGLAND GLASS CO.,
WM. L. LIBBEY, Agent.

BOSTON AND SANDWICH GLASS CO.,
SEWALL H. FESSENDEN, Agent.

UNION GLASS CO.,
J. P. GREGORY, Agent.

SUFFOLK GLASS CO.,
L. HODSDON, Agent.

Boston, May 1, 1875.

Collection of the author

PLATE 219

Poster Notice of a Trade Sale of Packages of Glass.

PLATE 220

Engraved ware, as shown in a Boston & Sandwich Glass Company catalogue.

PLATE 221

Dolphin epergne and two frosted glass classical figures supporting bowls which are engraved. Taken from a Boston & Sandwich Glass Company sales catalogue of the 1870's.

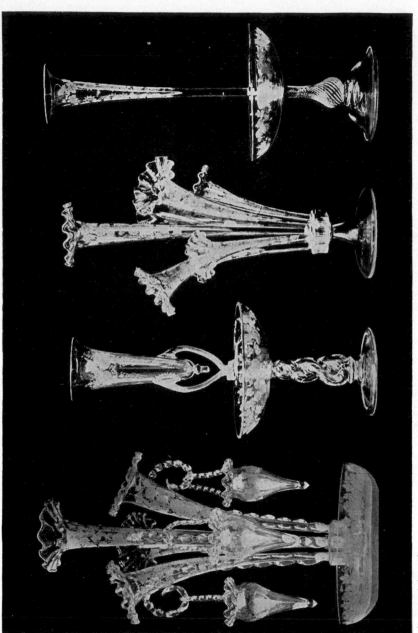

PLATE 222

Ornate blown and engraved epergnes, as shown in a Boston & Sandwich Glass Company catalogue.

PLATE 223

This type of decorated glassware is not usually associated with Sandwich but as documented by old catalogues, was made there in large quantities. It was probably inspired by contemporary English glass, generally attributed to Bristol.

PLATE 224

Page from an old Boston & Sandwich Glass Company catalogue. The water bottles with inverted tumblers seen at the upper right were known as "water bottles with tumble-ups."

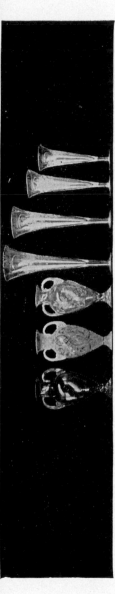

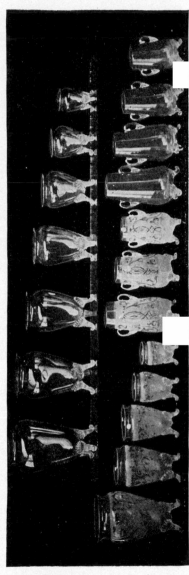

PLATE 225

Vases with applied ribbed feet were among items produced by the Boston & Sandwich Glass Company in the latter years in an attempt to meet Midwestern competition.

Boston, March 9, 1891.

A final dividend of One $\frac{50}{100}$ Dollars per share of the Capital Stock of the BOSTON & SANDWICH GLASS COMPANY will be paid on and after March 25, 1891, at the office of Gorham Rogers, Treasurer, No. 20 Federal Street, to Stockholders of record of March 9, upon the presentation and surrender of their Certificates of Stock, and upon said Stockholders signing an agreement, of which the following is a copy:

"Each of the undersigned persons, firms and corporations, hereby acknowledges to have received of the BOSTON & SANDWICH GLASS COMPANY, the sum hereunder set against his, her, or its name, being the final dividend of One $\frac{50}{100}$ Dollars per share of all the shares in said BOSTON & SANDWICH GLASS COMPANY, owned or held by such undersigned, and surrenders his, her, or its Certificates of Stock without being released from any liability because of such surrender."

Per order of the Directors.

GORHAM ROGERS, Treasurer.

PLATE 226

Final Dividend Notice of the Boston & Sandwich Glass Company. This printed notice of a dollar and a half a share and surrender of the stock is dated March 9, 1891, three years after the fires at the Sandwich plant had been extinguished.

PLATE 227

All that remains standing today of the Boston & Sandwich Glass Company.

INDEX

Index